X

lev 2.5
Enrlev (LG K-3)
.5

Seed to Plant

Kristin Baird Rattini

Washington, D.C.

To my roots: Mom, Dad, and Kim —K.B.R.

The publisher and author gratefully acknowledge the expert review of this book by horticulturist Gregg Henry Quinn.

Paperback ISBN: 978-1-4263-1470-4
Library edition ISBN: 978-1-4263-1471-1

Book design by YAY! Design

Cover (flower), cobalt88/Shutterstock; (seeds), Jiang Hongyan/Shutterstock; 1, Chris Hill/Shutterstock; 2, Digital Vision; 4 (UP), Laurie Campbell/naturepl.com; 4 (LO), Le Do/Shutterstock; 5 (UP), Valentyn Volkov/Shutterstock; 5 (LO), homydesign/Shutterstock; 6, AgStock Images/Corbis; 7 (UP), Visuals Unlimited/Getty Images; 7 (LO), Joshua Howard/National Geographic Creative; 8, Granger Wootz/Blend Images/Corbis; 9, Givaga/Shutterstock; 10 (UP), Kim Taylor/naturepl.com; 10 (CTR), Kim Taylor/naturepl.com; 10 (LO), Catalin Petolea/Shutterstock; 11, AgStock Images/Corbis; 12, MM Productions/Corbis; 13, Scott Stulberg/Corbis; 14–15 (background), oriontrail/Shutterstock; 14–15, Orla/Shutterstock; 16 (UP), Stephanie Pilick/dpa/Shutterstock; 16 (LOLE), Dieter Heinemann/Westend61/Corbis; 16–17 (background), lobster20/Shutterstock; 17 (UPLE), Olaf Simon/iStockphoto; 17 (CTR), Paolo Giocoso/Grand Tour/Corbis; 17 (LO), Palette7/Shutterstock; 18 (INSET both), Jill Fromer/E+/Getty Images; 18–19, Comstock Images/Getty Images; 20, Roel Dillen/iStockphoto/Getty Images; 21, Behzad Ghaffarian/National Geographic My Shot; 22 (LE), Ingram; 22 (RT), Gentl and Hyers/Botanica/Getty Images; 23 (LE), Alexo11973/Shutterstock; 23 (RT), mark higgins/Shutterstock; 24–25, Simon Bell/National Geographic My Shot; 24 (INSET), Raymond Barlow/National Geographic My Shot; 25 (INSET), Ints Vikmanis/Shutterstock; 26, Craig Lovell/Corbis; 27, Zurijeta/Shutterstock; 28, Alivepix/Shutterstock; 29 (1), Hamster-Man/Shutterstock; 29 (2), Mark Thiessen, NGS; 29 (3), Mark Thiessen, NGS; 29 (4), beyond fotomedia RF/Getty Images; 30 (LE), Sam Abell/National Geographic Creative; 30 (RT), Ingram; 31 (UPLE), Olaf Simon/iStockphoto; 31 (UPRT), Dmitry Naumov/Shutterstock; 31 (LOLE), Martin Ruegner/Digital Vision/Getty Images; 31 (LORT), Alexo11973/Shutterstock; 32 (UPLE), Kim Taylor/naturepl.com; 32 (LOLE), Anna Dimo/National Geographic My Shot; 32 (UPRT), irin-k/Shutterstock; 32 (LORT), udra11/Shutterstock; Buzz word bees, Angela Shvedova/Shutterstock; header banner, Kostenyukova Nataliya/Shutterstock

Printed in the United States of America
13/WOR/1

Table of Contents

What Is a Plant?

A plant is a living thing. It stays in one place. But it grows and changes, just like you.

white water lily

fern

tangerine tree

orchid

Plants can be
big or small.
Some have
flowers.
Others also
grow fruit.
Trees are
plants, too.

5

Plants are a big part of our world.
Farmers grow fruits and vegetables.
These plants give us food.

Q How is a tree like a big dog?

A They both have a lot of bark.

A farmer in his cotton field

Some plants can be used to make clothing. Your T-shirt is made from cotton plants.

Other plants are cozy homes for animals.

A bear in a tree

Parts of a Plant

You can use your body to remember the parts of a plant.

Arms are like leaves.

Your body is like a stem.

Feet are like roots.

Roots hold the plant in the ground. The stem helps the plant stand up tall. Leaves soak up the sunlight.

leaves

stem

roots

How Does a Plant Begin?

1 Let's dig in! Most plants start as a seed.

2 The seed splits open. A shoot pushes out. This is called germination (jur-muh-NAY-shun).

3 A new plant is beginning!

Buzz Words

GERMINATION: The sprouting of a new plant from a seed

SEEDLING: A young plant

A seedling starts to grow.
Roots reach down into the soil.
A stem pushes up into the air.

leaves

stem

roots

A Plant Grows

Watering a garden helps it grow.

Just like you, a plant grows
bigger and bigger. The roots spread
out and down into the soil.
The stem gets thicker and stronger.
More leaves and
branches grow.

Buzz Word

SOIL: The top layer
of earth, which
plants grow in

What Do Plants Need?

Plants need these things in order to grow:

- ✓ Soil
- ✓ Water
- ✓ Food
- ✓ Sunlight
- ✓ Air
- ✓ Space

Water and some food come from the soil. The roots soak them up.

Sunlight and air enter through the leaves. Plants use them to make more food. Plants also need space to grow.

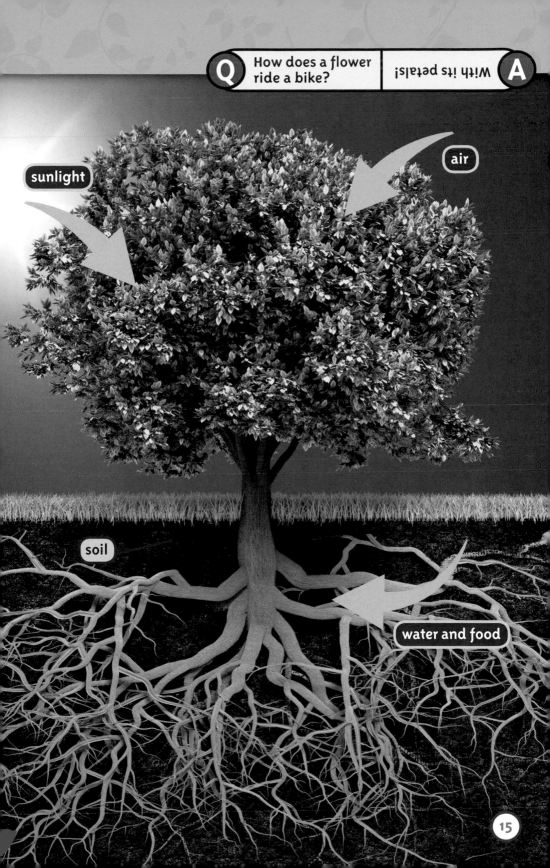

sunlight

air

soil

water and food

6 Fun Plant Facts

1

This palm tree seed can weigh as much as a fourth grader. It's the heaviest seed in the world.

2

Scrub-a-dub in the tub! Plants are used in many soaps and shampoos.

3

Flowers Bloom

Many plants grow flowers.

They start as a bump called a bud.

The bud slowly opens. Petals gently unfold.

Surprise! It's a flower.

The paper for this book was made from trees.

4

One sunflower can make as many as 1,000 seeds!

5

Bamboo grows the fastest of any plant. It can grow as tall as a three-year-old kid in one day!

6

The tallest living tree is taller than the Statue of Liberty, in New York, U.S.A.

Flowers Bloom

Many plants grow flowers.

They start as a bump called a bud.

The bud slowly opens. Petals gently unfold.

Q What did one flower say to another?

A Hi, bud!

Surprise!
It's a flower.

19

Sticky Pollen

Flowers make a sticky powder called pollen.

Pollen sticks to birds and bees when they fly from flower to flower.

Then the pollen rubs off on other flowers. This is called pollination (POL-uh-NAY-shun). It helps flowers make seeds!

Buzz Word

POLLINATION: The moving of pollen from one flower to another. This makes seeds grow.

21

Seeds

Plants keep seeds in different places.

Many plants grow a case around the seeds. The case is called a pod. Peas and maple tree seeds grow in pods.

maple tree pod

pea pod

seeds

seeds

Orange seeds are different. Their seeds are on the inside.

seeds

seeds

But strawberry seeds are on the outside.

Now the seeds
take a trip.
Some float
on the wind.
Others are
carried away
by animals.

A bird carries a berry
with a seed inside.

The seeds
fall to the
ground.
Soon they
sprout, or germinate.
A new plant begins.

A squirrel holds a large seed.

Dandelion seeds scatter in the wind.

Pass the Plants, Please!

People and animals eat plants to stay healthy. How many plants did you eat today?

A panda eats a bamboo plant.

Watermelon is a fruit that comes from a plant.

Make Your Garden Grow

You can grow your own bean plant. Ask a grown-up for help.

You'll need:

✓ One lima bean seed
✓ A cup of water
✓ A 4-inch flowerpot, glass jar, or paper cup
✓ Soil

1 Soak your seed in a cup of water overnight.

2 Fill the flowerpot with soil. Push your seed down into the soil about one inch.

3 Add a little water to moisten the soil.

4 Place the pot in a warm, sunny spot. Add a little water whenever the soil gets dry. Your seedling should sprout within one week!

What in the World?

These pictures show close-up views of things in this book. Use the hints below to figure out what's in the pictures. Answers are on page 31.

HINT: This opens into a flower.

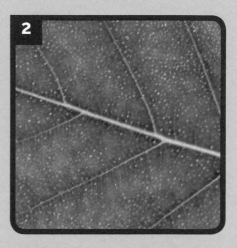

HINT: This part of a plant takes in sunlight and air.

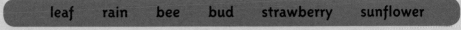

leaf   rain   bee   bud   strawberry   sunflower

HINT: This flower can make up to 1,000 seeds.

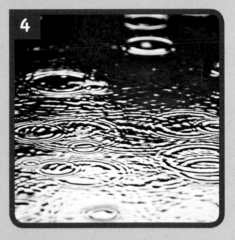

HINT: This falls and waters the plants.

HINT: This buzzes as it flies from flower to flower.

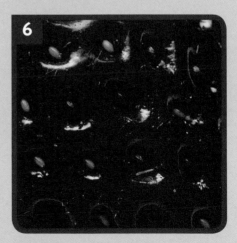

HINT: This has seeds on the outside.

Answers: 1. bud, 2. leaf, 3. sunflower, 4. rain, 5. bee, 6. strawberry

GERMINATION: The sprouting of a new plant from a seed

POLLINATION: The moving of pollen from one flower to another. This makes seeds grow.

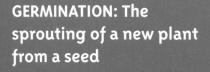

SEEDLING: A young plant

SOIL: The top layer of earth, which plants grow in